HOW & WHY?

SPIDERS SPIN SILK

Elaine Pascoe is the author of more than 20 acclaimed children's books on a wide range of subjects.
Dwight Kuhn's scientific expertise and artful eye work together with the camera to capture the awesome wonder of the natural world.

Please visit our web site at: www.garethstevens.com
For a free color catalog describing Gareth Stevens Publishing's list of high-quality books
and multimedia programs, call 1-800-542-2595 or fax your request to (414) 332-3567.

Library of Congress Cataloging-in-Publication Data

Pascoe, Elaine.
      Spiders spin silk / by Elaine Pascoe; photographs by Dwight Kuhn. — North American ed.
           p. cm. — (How & why: a springboards into science series)
      Includes bibliographical references and index.
      Summary: Briefly explains how spiders make silk and use it in various ways.
      ISBN 0-8368-3013-X (lib. bdg.)
      1. Spider webs—Juvenile literature. [1. Spider webs. 2. Spiders.] I. Kuhn, Dwight, ill. II. Title.
      QL458.4.P365   2002
      595.4'4—dc21   2001049487

This North American edition first published in 2002 by
Gareth Stevens Publishing
A World Almanac Education Group Company
330 West Olive Street, Suite 100
Milwaukee, WI 53212 USA

First published in the United States in 2000 by Creative Teaching Press, Inc., P.O. Box 2723, Huntington Beach, CA 92647-0723.
Text © 2000 by Elaine Pascoe; photographs © 2000 by Dwight Kuhn. Additional end matter © 2002 by Gareth Stevens, Inc.

Gareth Stevens editor: Mary Dykstra
Gareth Stevens designer: Tammy Gruenewald

Printed in the United States of America

1 2 3 4 5 6 7 8 9 06 05 04 03 02

HOW&WHY?

SPIDERS SPIN SILK

by Elaine Pascoe
photographs by Dwight Kuhn

Gareth Stevens Publishing
A WORLD ALMANAC EDUCATION GROUP COMPANY

A garden spider weaves a web of silky threads. When the web is covered with dew, it looks like a diamond necklace.

A jumping spider spins a silk anchor line. The thread looks fragile, but it is very strong. Spiders make many kinds of silk, and they use their silk in many ways.

A garden spider's web is a deadly insect trap. When an insect, such as this grasshopper, blunders into the web, it gets caught in the sticky silk threads. Then the hungry spider rushes over and wraps its prey in sheets of silk.

The silk is made by glands in the spider's belly. It comes out through openings called spinnerets. All spiders have spinnerets, and all spiders make silk.

A jumping spider pounces on its prey like a cat. As the spider leaps, its silk anchor line trails behind it. The silk is liquid when it comes out, but it dries immediately.

The anchor line is stronger than steel wire and is firmly fastened to an object, such as a flower. When the spider misses its target, it does not fall very far. The anchor line catches it, and the spider climbs back up the anchor line to the flower.

Many spiders use silk to make nests. A silky nest is a safe place for a spider to hide.

Have you ever seen a house spider's nest? There might be one in your house! This spider's nest is a messy tangle of silk. The house spider is not a very neat housekeeper!

The crab spider has no nest. It waits for insects on a flower. When a bee comes looking for nectar, the crab spider rushes over to it and bites it. The crab spider's bite is poisonous, and the bee stops moving.

Then the spider pumps juices into the bee. The juices turn the insect into a kind of bee soup, and the spider sucks it up. A crab spider does not use silk to catch its prey, but, like most spiders, it uses silk for many other purposes.

A female spider wraps her eggs in sheets of soft silk. Then she bundles the silk-wrapped eggs into a round egg sac. Many female spiders stay near their eggs to guard them.

The wolf spider's egg sac is attached to her spinnerets. She carries it wherever she goes.

The garden spider uses strong strands of silk to fasten her egg sac to a plant. The eggs stay on the plant through winter, safe in their silky case.

Young spiders hatch inside the egg sac. In early spring, they leave the egg sac and spin silk of their own.

Can you answer these "HOW & WHY" questions?

1. Why does a garden spider spin a web?

2. How does a spider make silk?

3. How does silk keep a jumping spider from falling?

4. How does a crab spider catch prey?

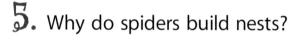
5. Why do spiders build nests?

6. How do spiders use silk to protect their eggs?

(See page 20 for answers.)

ANSWERS

1. A garden spider spins a sticky, silk web to catch its prey.

2. A spider's silk is produced by glands in the spider's belly and comes out through openings called spinnerets.

3. A jumping spider spins a silk anchor line that stays attached to its body as it pounces and keeps the spider from falling very far.

4. A crab spider hides on a flower, and when an insect lands on the flower, the spider rushes over to the prey and pumps poisonous juices into it.

5. Spiders build nests so they will have safe places to hide.

6. Female spiders wrap their eggs with soft silk, which holds the eggs together in a protective egg sac.

Preserve a Web

With an adult's help, look for a spiderweb in your backyard or in a nearby field. If there is no spider on the web, spray the web with nonaerosol hair spray, starting at the center of the web and moving outward. Hold a piece of black construction paper or poster board behind the web, moving the paper forward until the web touches it. When the web is completely on the paper, cut the lines anchoring the web and carefully remove it. Let the web dry, then study its structure to learn more about amazing spiders.

Spinning Tales

Pick one of the spiders in this book and write a story about a day in that spider's life. You could pretend you are the spider writing in a journal or a diary before going to sleep. Try to imagine all the things that might happen to a spider throughout the day. Use crayons or markers to draw pictures that illustrate your story or journal entry.

An Eggs-tra Special Spider

Ask an adult to help you cut out one section of a cardboard egg carton. Paint this section with black acrylic paint to make it look like the body of a spider. Using the tip of a scissors, carefully poke four holes into each side of the spider's body. Cut four black pipe cleaners in half to make eight legs, then stick the end of each leg into a different hole on the spider's body. Bend the pipe cleaners to make the spider stand. If you have them, add jiggly eyes to your special spider.

GLOSSARY

anchor line: the line of silk some spiders produce and attach to an object to help keep them from falling too far as they move from place to place.

blunders (v): makes a foolish mistake.

bundles (v): gathers in a group that is tied or wrapped together in some way.

dew: droplets of water that form on cool surfaces, such as grass, during the night.

egg sac: a pouchlike container a spider makes to protect its eggs until they hatch.

fastened: joined to or attached.

fragile: delicate; easy to break or to damage.

glands: parts of an animal's body that produce liquids for particular uses.

nectar: the sweet liquid in flowers that many insects and birds like to eat.

poisonous: able to cause sickness or injury and sometimes even death.

pounces: jumps very suddenly at or on top of something, such as prey.

prey (n): animals hunted and killed by other animals for food.

silk: fine threads produced by a spider and used to build its web.

spinnerets: the special parts of spiders' bodies that produce silk.

strands (n): thin, threadlike pieces of materials such as fibers, wire, or hair.

tangle (n): a knotted, twisted, or snarled mass of material.

trails (v): comes along or drags behind.

weaves: passes threads or thin strips over and under each other to hold them in place.

More Books to Read

Jumping Spiders. Life Cycles (series). David M. Schwartz (Gareth Stevens)

Outside and Inside Spiders. Sandra Markle (Aladdin)

Sophie's Masterpiece: A Spider's Tale. Eileen Spinelli (Simon & Schuster)

Spectacular Spiders. Linda Glaser (Millbrook Press)

Spider's Lunch: All about Garden Spiders. Joanna Cole (Grosset & Dunlap)

Spiders Spin Webs. Yvonne Winer (Econo-Clad Books)

Videos

Bug City: Spiders & Scorpions. (Schlessinger Media)

The Magic School Bus Spins a Web: The Special Ways of Spiders. (Scholastic)

See How They Grow: Insects and Spiders. (Sony Wonder)

Web Sites

homepage.powerup.com.au/~glen/spider.htm

www.billybear4kids.com/butterfly/spiders/information.html

www.stemnet.nf.ca/CITE/spiderswebs.htm

Some web sites stay current longer than others. For additional web sites, use a good search engine to locate the following topics: *spider silk, spiders, spiderwebs,* and *spinnerets.*

INDEX